DESTINATION

Middle Ages

Your Guide to
The Arts in the
Middle Ages

Cynthia O'Brien

Crabtree Publishing Company
www.crabtreebooks.com

Crabtree Publishing Company
www.crabtreebooks.com

Author: Cynthia O'Brien

Managing Editor: Tim Cooke

Designer: Lynne Lennon

Picture Manager: Sophie Mortimer

Design Manager: Keith Davis

Editorial Director: Lindsey Lowe

Children's Publisher: Anne O'Daly

Editor: Petrice Custance

Proofreader: Wendy Scavuzzo

Production coordinator
and prepress technician: Tammy McGarr

Print coordinator: Margaret Amy Salter

Written and produced for Crabtree Publishing Company
by Brown Bear Books

Photographs (t=top, b=bottom, l=left, r=right, c=center):
Front Cover: Getty Images: Leemage tr; **HLLF – Petit de Jullevelle:** cr; **Shutterstock:** Mehmet Cetin br; **Thinkstock:** Steve Allen Photo main.

Interior: Alamy: 21b,Neil McAllister 19b; **Bridgeman Art Library:** 16r, 21t, Tallandier 28l; **British Library:** 10bl, 18tr; **Castres Bibliotheque Municipale:** 19t; **Dreamstime:** 23br; **Getty Images:** Alinari Archives/CORBIS 11bl, DEA/Agli Orti 9tr, 27l, Fine Art Images/Heritage Images 9bl; **Library of Congress:** 20tl; **Savage McKay:** 32bl; **Metropolitan Museum of Art:** 4, 12, 25; **Public Domain:** Didier B 15tl, Gallica/Evrard d'Espinques 8, Milkbreath 24l; **Shutterstock:** Ramon Antonio 13b, Zvonimir Atletic 14, Anatolijs Laicans 23tr, Kasenia Palimski 13t, Production Perig 10-11t, Bill Perry 22, Renata Sedmakova 15b, Smereka 29br; **SuperStock:** 24br; **Thinkstock:** istockphoto 8bl, 17bc, 20br, 28br, Photos.com 16bl, 18bl, 25br, Jan Schneckenhaus 29l; **Topfoto:** 27br, World History Archive 5b, 26; **Uffizi Gallery:** 17l.

All other photos, artwork and maps, **Brown Bear Books**.

Brown Bear Books has made every attempt to contact the copyright holder. If you have any information please contact licensing@brownbearbooks.co.uk

Library and Archives Canada Cataloguing in Publication

O'Brien, Cynthia (Cynthia J.), author
    Your guide to the arts in the Middle Ages / Cynthia O'Brien.

(Destination: Middle Ages)
Includes index.
Issued in print and electronic formats.
ISBN 978-0-7787-2995-2 (hardcover).--
ISBN 978-0-7787-3002-6 (softcover).--
ISBN 978-1-4271-1868-4 (HTML)

    1. Arts, Medieval--Juvenile literature. 2. Art, Medieval--Juvenile literature. 3. Literature, Medieval--Juvenile literature. 4. Architecture, Medieval--Juvenile literature. I. Title.

NX449.O27 2017   j709.02   C2016-907399-8
                                      C2016-907400-5

Library of Congress Cataloging-in-Publication Data

CIP is Available at the Library of Congress

Crabtree Publishing Company
www.crabtreebooks.com   1-800-387-7650   Printed in Canada/032017/BF20170111

Published in Canada
Crabtree Publishing
616 Welland Ave.
St. Catharines, ON
L2M 5V6

Published in the United States
Crabtree Publishing
PMB 59051
350 Fifth Avenue, 59th Floor
New York, New York 10118

Published in the United Kingdom
Crabtree Publishing
Maritime House
Basin Road North, Hove
BN41 1WR

Published in Australia
Crabtree Publishing
3 Charles Street
Coburg North
VIC, 3058

Contents

Before We Start

The creations of medieval artists range from cathedrals to paintings, music, and poetry. Artistic works are one of our main tools for understanding life in the Middle Ages.

ART OF POETRY

✦ Superstar poets

Poetry was the most popular form of writing in the Middle Ages. Poets such as Geoffrey Chaucer and Dante Alighieri were well known. Some poems were **lyrics** with short rhyming verses about emotions. Other poems were longer works. Ballads told a story in a series of short verses. Epics told stories about heroes in long, unbroken-verse narratives.

A RELIGIOUS AGE

+ **Christianity rules!**

+ **The Church supports the arts**

After the fall of the Roman Empire in 476, the Roman Catholic Church became very powerful in Europe. Most Europeans shared the Catholic faith, and the arts reflected this devotion. Christian symbols, stories, and saints were the subjects of paintings and sculptures. **Scribes** wrote and illustrated, by hand, decorated versions of the Bible (right) and other religious books, such as collections of prayers. Choirs sang unaccompanied sacred songs, or **plainchants**, to honor God.

THE GREAT MONASTERIES
✦ Homes of monks and nuns

Medieval monasteries served many purposes. Monks helped the poor and the sick. They were also teachers and artists. In the days before books could be printed, monks copied them out by hand (left). **Orders** of monks were influential and wealthy. Many of these orders were **patrons** of the arts.

TAKING CARE OF BUSINESS

☞ Guilds control trades

rganizations called guilds controlled the trade and afts in a town or city. Craftsmen such as artists d wood carvers belonged to guilds that tried to ntrol standards of work. The guilds grew wealthy d built large headquarters for themselves (right). uild members gained social status and job security.

A WORLD OF MUSIC

+ Choirs and minstrels

In the early Middle Ages, church choirs sang simple chants. Later, composers wrote music that was more melodic and often accompanied by instruments. Popular instruments included the stringed lute and viol (left). The sackbut was a brass instrument with a slide, like a modern trombone. Secular, or non-religious, music was popular. Minstrels were traveling musicians. They played music to entertain people in the street, or in their homes.

Where in the World?

Much artistic, literary, and musical creation in the Middle Ages was concentrated in particular areas. However, ideas spread widely through a network of traveling scholars, merchants, and monks.

Ireland
Around the year 800, monks in Ireland copied out by hand the four gospels of the Bible. Known as *The Book of Kells*, its decorative illustrations make it one of the most spectacular manuscripts created during the Middle Ages.

IRELAND

GERMANY

EUROPE

Paris

FRANCE

ITALY

Florence

SPAIN

Córdoba

AFRICA

Córdoba
Córdoba in Spain was the home to a mosque with spectacular decorated arches. Spain was a main route through which Islamic artistic influences reached the rest of Europe.

Paris
Paris was a cultural center of the Middle Ages. In 1137, it was home to the first appearance of the Gothic style of architecture. Featuring delicate columns, **flying buttresses**, and pointed arches, the Gothic style became favored for cathedrals throughout Europe.

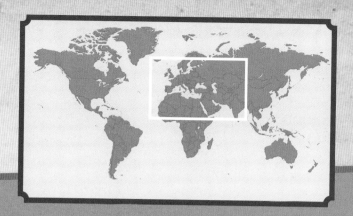

Gutenberg
Around 1450, the German printer Johannes Gutenberg invented Europe's first printing press. The invention made producing books far cheaper and quicker, and led to a huge increase in the number of books in Europe.

Florence
Florence in Tuscany, Italy, was one of the centers of the **Renaissance**. This artistic movement, which began around 1200, was based on a rediscovery of classical learning from ancient Greece and Rome. It placed a new importance on the thoughts and feelings of the individual, rather than the lessons of the Bible.

RUSSIA

IRAN

Shiraz

Shiraz
Shiraz in Persia (modern-day Iran) was home to the great Persian poet Hafiz. It was also a center of Islamic artistic production, noted for its woven carpets and decorated tiles.

New Names
This map shows the modern names of countries. Most of these states did not exist in the Middle Ages.

Who We'll Meet

Most early medieval artists did not sign their work. Later in the period, some painters, architects, and poets did begin to identify their work. Many became well known.

On Artists

The Renaissance was the first time artists became famous. People wrote books about their lives and works. That is how we know so much about them today.

A MYSTERY MAN

✦ First tales of King Arthur

Between 1165 and 1180, French writer Chrétien de Troyes wrote many poems. Much of Chrétien's life is a mystery, but his writings were popular. In particular, Chrétien wrote **romances**. His most famous works told tales about the **legendary** King Arthur and his court. Chrétien's poems described Arthur's court at Camelot and the adventures of the knights of the Round Table (right).

BREAKING NEWS

Reports from Italy say the architect Filippo Brunelleschi has built a remarkable new dome. The dome is part of the Duomo, or cathedral, in Florence (left). Born in 1377, Brunelleschi trained as a sculptor and goldsmith. He became an architect later in his life, and started designing the dome for the Duomo in his 40s.

CLASSICAL POET

- ☞ **Learning from the past**
- ☞ **Revisiting the classics**

Francesco Petrarca (right), known as Petrarch, was an Italian poet born in 1304. As a child, he was fascinated by the literature of ancient Greece and Rome. At 16, he joined a religious order, but still traveled, studied literature, and began to write poetry. His poems were very popular. He wrote **sonnets** about a woman he met named Laura, even though he rarely spoke to her. Petrarch became Rome's **poet laureate** in 1341.

A REMARKABLE WOMAN

- + **Hildegard composes, writes, and paints...**
- + **...oh, and she's a saint!**

Born to a noble German family, Hildegard of Bingen (left) was unusual for medieval times. She was one of the few women writers, but she also composed music and poetry. Hildegard became a nun at age 18 and went on to found two monasteries. She wrote about her religious visions and what they meant. She also wrote plays, as well as songs and poems. Pope Benedict XVI canonized Hildegard in 2012, making her a saint.

MUSIC MAKER

- ✦ **Thomas writes church music**
- ✦ **First music in print**

Little is known about the early life of Thomas Tallis. The English composer wrote church music. In 1575, Queen Elizabeth I gave Tallis and composer William Byrd the right to publish their music. This was the first time music was printed. Tallis's piece for 40 voices (*Spem in alium*) singing different parts is still popular today.

A Little Bit of History

People, ideas, and innovation spread widely in the Middle Ages. There were great achievements in the arts and sciences. The changes taking place transformed how people saw the world around them.

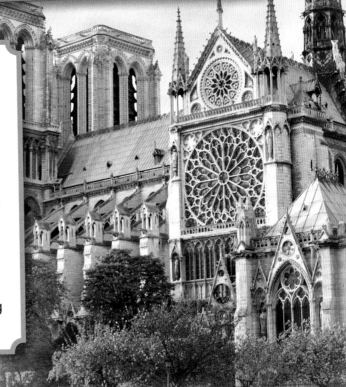

THE GREAT CATHEDRALS
✦ Wonders for worship

Christianity inspired many artistic achievements in the Middle Ages. They included the building of great cathedrals in important towns. Cathedrals were large churches. The first cathedrals were built in the "Romanesque" style. They had thick, heavy walls and round arches. Later cathedrals were tall and flooded with light. They had soaring towers, called steeples.

A NEW PHILOSOPHY

+ Humanism gives a new focus...

+ ...makes things more "human!"

Humanism developed in Italy in the late Middle Ages. T way of thinking said that human behavior and reason w more important than ideas about the world based only religion. Medieval humanists based their **philosophy** on men and their achievements. But they encouraged peop to question old ideas. The female writer Christine de Pisa (left) wrote books to show how women had also achieve many important things in the past.

BREAKING NEWS

Have you noticed a new change in drawing? The Italian architect Filippo Brunelleschi has developed a technique called linear **perspective**. It creates an illusion that a scene or object is three-dimensional. Artists such as Paolo Uccello are busy trying it out by painting buildings with many straight lines and grids (left).

Did you know?

In the 700s, some people felt icons, or images of holy figures, made people worship objects instead of God. So they destroyed many paintings and sculptures in churches.

UNITING EUROPE

+ **Charlemagne is Holy Roman Emperor**
+ **New interest in learning**

In 800, Charlemagne became the Holy Roman emperor. As king of the Franks, he fought for years to unite Europe and convert its different peoples to Christianity. Charlemagne was passionate about education, and promoted a renewed interest in learning and culture.

REVISITING THE CLASSICS

☞ **Learning from Greece and Rome**

The term "classical" refers to ancient Greece and Rome. After the fall of Rome, much classical learning was forgotten in Europe. In the later Middle Ages, this learning was reintroduced from the Islamic world and Turkey. Europeans were impressed by the stories, ideas, and use of language in classical works. Writers wrote versions of classical stories, and artists painted scenes from classical works.

My Medieval Journal

Filippo Brunelleschi's rules for linear perspective made it possible for artists to draw objects that appear to be three-dimensional. Use the Internet to research some of the basic rules of perspective, and try using them in an artwork of your own.

Art and Entertainment

Medieval art was everywhere in the shape of paintings, tapestries, and furniture. Great cathedrals were full of artworks, and actors and musicians could be seen performing outdoors in the streets.

MUSIC ALL AROUND

+ Music for eating...

+ ...and music for dancing

Music played an important part in medieval life, from large towns and royal courts to small villages. In the great hall of a palace, musicians played while everyone ate dinner. At town festivals, people gathered to celebrate with music and dancing. Europeans often played instruments that had come from Asia, including the lute and the viol. They had learned about these instruments from Muslims in the Middle East.

PORTABLE PAINTING

✦ If you like your picture...

✦ ...carry it with you!

Paintings were valuable objects. People who owned paintings took them with them if they traveled. Medieval artists created moveable panel paintings and **altarpieces** on wood. Often, altarpieces were triptychs, which were three panels hinged together (above). The panels could be folded shut to protect the painting if it was moved from the altar for safety, or taken to be displayed in another church.

NEWS FROM AFAR

Wealthy Europeans who could afford them bought carpets from the Middle East. Merchants brought brightly colored wool and silk rugs and carpets from Persia. Some people hung beautiful rugs on the wall rather than putting them on the floor. Home decorating was popular among royalty and wealthy merchants. They owned large **tapestries**, beautiful books, and pieces of art. Displaying these items in the home declared someone's status in society.

ARTISTS IN WOOD

- ☛ **Carved furniture**
- ☛ **Painted sculptures**

Many medieval sculptors worked in wood. They carved decorations, figures, and other forms using axes, chisels, and other tools. Woodcarving became very popular in the 1300s, and artists always painted their sculptures until the 1400s. Sculptors decorated the interiors of many churches. They also carved chairs, pews (below), and statues.

PLAY TIME

- **+ Plays on carts...**
- **+ ...but drama is a serious business**

amas were popular in the Middle Ages. ere were no theaters, so plays were formed in houses or inns. Some plays re even staged on the back of carts! ere were three kinds of plays, which re all entertaining, but they also had erious message. Mystery plays were mas that told stories from the Bible. acle plays depicted the lives of istian saints. They were very popular rance. Morality plays appeared in the r Middle Ages. They were about the iggle between good and evil.

Serving the Church

The Christian church was central to European medieval life. Designers, stonemasons, painters, and others worked to decorate cathedrals inside and out.

Frescoes

Frescoes adorned church walls. Artists painted pictures directly onto wet plaster. The images became part of the plaster as it dried.

TO THE GLORY OF GOD

+ Cathedral builders show devotion...

+ ...by working for years!

Helping to build a church was an honor for medieval craftsmen. Using their skills in this way showed their religious devotion. Building a cathedral took hundreds of workers many years. For example, work began on the Notre-Dame Cathedral in Paris in 1163. It was completed in 1345—nearly 200 years later!

A VISUAL FEAST

✦ Look around in church...

✦ ...there's always plenty to see!

Cathedrals and churches were full of images tellin stories from the Bible. Sculptors such as Giovanni Pisano carved elaborate designs, figures, and scenes (above). Paintings covered the walls. As ar became more realistic, sculptures began to inclu life-sized figures, such as the Madonna and child. Later, stained-glass windows also portrayed Bible scenes. The windows flooded cathedrals with ligh

SENDING A MESSAGE

- ☛ Teaching the faith
- ☛ Visual communications

People who could not read or write learned the Bible stories from paintings, stained glass, and sculpture in churches. The church of Sainte-Chapelle, in Paris, has huge stained glass windows (left). They show scenes from the Old and New Testaments.

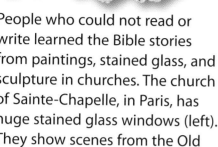

MY MEDIEVAL JOURNAL

In a stained-glass window, a scene is depicted in a mosaic of small pieces of colored glass held together by thin black strips of lead. Draw a design for your own stained-glass window to illustrate a scene from school or home. Then color it in.

REMEMBERING THE DEAD

✦ Decorated tombs

ich, powerful, or holy people were buried inside the hurch. The tombs were decorated with carved ffigies. The carvings showed the dead person as hough he or she were lying asleep on top of the tomb.

FAVORITE SUBJECTS

+ Telling stories

Most medieval art focused on religious themes. Many artists chose scenes from the life of Christ, such as the famous *The Last Supper* (below) by Leonardo da Vinci. People learned the stories from the paintings.

Patrons and Creators

Medieval artists and architects relied on wealthy people and institutions to pay for their works. Their patrons ranged from kings, nobles, and the wealthy, to the Catholic Church.

GUIDE BOOKS

+ If you're creating art...

+ ...follow these patterns

Medieval illustrators did not paint from life or nature. Instead, they copied images and lettering from pattern books. The books were full of designs and drawings that artists or sculptors could use for guidance, depending on what they required. Giovannino de Grassi's pattern book was particularly prized for its realistic drawings of subjects such as animals (right). De Grassi drew some images from life, but he also copied others from older pattern books.

WHO'S PAYING THE BILL?

✦ Noble patrons fund artists

Individual patrons were usually nobles or wealthy merchants. One notable patron was Jean de Berry, a French duke who was the brother of King Charles V. The duke collected beautiful jewelry and **manuscripts** (left). He commissioned tapestries and paintings, and he had castles built that were decorated with stained glass and sculpture.

IN THE STUDIO

✦ **Learning by example**

✦ **Apprentices train on the job**

n artist or craftsman was often assisted by several pprentices. From the age of about 12, these young eople lived with a master at his studio and worked r him. At first, an apprentice did basic tasks, such as eaning brushes. Over time, he or she learned the art r craft from the master. The artists' guild decided hen an apprentice was ready to become a master.

My Medieval Journal

Medieval apprentices often had to do the most boring chores in an artist's studio for many years. What sort of arguments would you use to persuade a friend who wanted to be an artist that being an apprentice was worthwhile?

GET IN THE PICTURE

☞ **Put yourself in a great painting**

Patrons often asked artists to include them in pictures. For example, an artist might include a portrait of a patron as a bystander at a biblical event. In *The Adoration of the Magi* by Sandro Botticelli (left), three members of the Medici family, the rulers of Florence, kneel in front of the Virgin Mary and baby Jesus. Two more members of the family are in the crowd. This reminded people who had paid for the painting. It was also seen as a sign of the patron's religious devotion.

NEWS FROM AFAR

A painter's pigments, or colors, came from a range of sources. The source of one bright blue was a stone called lapis lazuli (right), which was ground into a powder. Lapis lazuli could only be found in Afghanistan, in Central Asia, so it was very expensive. It was only used for the most important parts of a painting, such as the blue clothes of the Virgin Mary.

Shepherd Boy

The artist Giotto was once a shepherd. He is said to have become an apprentice after a traveler saw him drawing on rocks with charcoal.

World of Words

Monasteries were essential for literacy in the Middle Ages. Monks copied and illustrated holy books, and monasteries had large libraries. They were also centers for teaching literacy to the population.

IT'S ALL ILLUMINATED!

☞ Books are handwritten

Hand-written books are called manuscripts. The word comes from the Latin words *manus*, meaning "hand," and *scriptus*, meaning "to write." In the Middle Ages, scribes wrote and copied books by hand on prepared animal skin called vellum, or on paper called parchment. Some manuscripts were illuminated, or illustrated. An artist decorated capital letters or the margins of the pages with patterns and paintings, often using gold and silver.

THE BOOK ROOM

+ Monks at work

+ Copying old books

Monasteries often had a special room for monks to work on books. In this room, called a *scriptorium*, monks copied and illustrated books by hand. The scribes usually worked in strict silence. Some famous manuscripts involved more than one scribe. Three artists and four scribes probably worked on *The Book of Kells*, an illuminated manuscript from the 800s (left).

Teaching

Monasteries were centers of learning. Monks taught children to read (below). Students learned by repeating lessons out loud.

SPREADING THE WORD

✦ **Monks need to read**

✦ **Latin gives way to English**

Monks and nuns learned to read or write to study the Bible. Nobles also often had some education. At first, most books were written in Latin—the language used by the Church. In time, more books appeared in French, English, and other languages. With the founding of universities and secular schools, **literacy** spread.

> " *While I wrote I froze, and what I could not write by the beams of the sun I finished by candlelight.* "
>
> **A monk's complaint in the margin of a manuscript**

LIBRARIES OF LEARNING

☛ **Books so valuable...**

☛ **...they are chained to shelves**

...st people did not own books, which were ...pensive and rare. Libraries were therefore ...y important for reading and studying. ...ly monasteries had libraries of religious ...d classical books and writings. Monasteries ...red their books so that other scribes could ...py them. University libraries collected books ... a wider range of subjects, introducing law, ...nce, and other topics. The books were ...ached to the shelves by chains (right) so that ...one could take them out of the library.

A Poetic Age

Ballads

Ballads were long poems with many short verses. They told stories of adventures and real-life heroes. They were a popular form of entertainment.

The most popular form of medieval literature was poetry. There were many different forms of poetry. Poems told stories, taught lessons, and entertained.

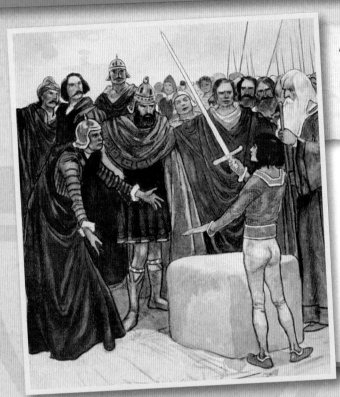

TALES OF ARTHUR

+ Popular legends

Geoffrey of Monmouth was a cleric who first made the legend of King Arthur famous. The first edition of his book, *The History of the Kings of Britain*, appeared around 1136. Geoffrey's tales of Arthur and his adventures fascinated readers in Europe. Arthur was said to have become king by pulling a sword from a stone where it had been stuck (left). Geoffrey also wrote another poem, *The Life of Merlin*, adding to Arthur's story. Both works influenced later poems and stories about Arthur.

SPIRITUAL JOURNEY

☞ Dante's poem might be a comedy...

☞ ...but people are saying it's divine!

The Italian poet Dante Alighieri's *The Divine Comedy* is an **epic** poem that describes an imaginary journey through Hell, **Purgatory**, and Heaven. On the way, Dante (right) meets all sorts of people, from sinners to saints. In spite of its title, Dante's poem is not funny. In the terms of classical poetry, a comedy is any work that begins bleakly and ends happily.

NEWS FROM AFAR

Hafiz (right) was born in Shiraz, in present-day Iran, in 1326. He wrote lyric poems about spirituality, politics, and love. Hafiz used a Persian form of poetry, the *ghazal*. A ghazal is a short rhyming poem with a set number of verses. It is usually about love. Hafiz wrote about 500 ghazals, including *Dīvān*, and became very famous. He remains Iran's most popular poet today.

TELLING TALES

✦ Pilgrims tell stories...

✦ ...and Chaucer writes them down

Geoffrey Chaucer was an English poet. Born to a merchant family, Chaucer was a soldier and later a member of the King's court. Chaucer's *The Canterbury Tales* is a collection of 24 long poems. The tales are often humorous stories told by **pilgrims** on their way from London, England, to a shrine in Canterbury 60 miles (96 km) away. Chaucer did not use academic language or Latin. He wrote in the form of plain English used in London. This, and an entertaining style, made Chaucer's works very popular.

> " *For I have learned that every heart will get What it prays for Most.* "
>
> **Hafiz**

MY MEDIEVAL JOURNAL

Chaucer's pilgrims tell one another stories to pass the time on the long journey to Canterbury. What sort of stories do you think would help make a journey pass more quickly? Give reasons for your answer.

Islamic Art

Muslim artists created unique art, from knotted carpets to grand mosques. European artists soon copied parts of Islamic style, such as the geometric patterns and swirling lines of Arabic lettering.

CARPETS AND TILES

+ Islamic decoration

+ Riot of color

Muslim artists made highly decorated tiles and rugs by hand. Tiles adorned Islamic buildings inside and out. Tile makers used different glazes and techniques to produce a range of colors. Luster glazes turned gold or silver. Sometimes, artists cut tiles into small pieces to make mosaics. Carpet makers knotted strands of wool and silk to create complicated patterns as they wove.

NEWS FROM AFAR

Mosques are religious buildings where Muslims gather to pray. They are also places of learning, and often spectacular to look at. The prayer hall of the Great Mosque of Córdoba, in Spain, has 856 columns holding up hundreds of arches (above). Artists carved patterns into stone and wood, and covered the walls with painted and glazed tiles and mosaics. The mosque of Bibi-Khanum, in Uzbekistan, still retains its bright colors.

THE ART OF DECORATION

☞ **Religious rules...**

☞ **...and ways to overcome them**

According to Islamic rules, Muslim artists could not portray living things. So instead of painting people or animals, they created beautiful, intricate patterns. The most important patterns were based on **calligraphy,** or decorative handwriting. Other patterns were known as arabesque. This style featured plant patterns or **geometric** shapes (right). The designs seem to repeat endlessly. This reflects the Muslim belief in the infinite presence of Allah, or God.

IN THE GARDEN

✦ **Models of paradise**

✦ **Plenty of water**

Gardens were important in Islam, because they were seen as a recreation of paradise. Islamic gardens followed a geometric plan, such as the *chahar bagh*. This type of walled garden was divided into four parts by water channels (below). Often, a fountain was placed at the center.

THE ISLAMIC INFLUENCE

✦ **A rich legacy for the West**

Islam had a great impact on medieval Europe. Wealthy Europeans bought imported Islamic textiles, ceramics, and other artworks for their homes. Islamic script, patterns, and colors inspired Europe's artists and architects. The pointed Gothic arch is also inspired by Islamic design. It was widely used in Europe's cathedrals (right).

Painters and Architects

The Middle Ages saw sweeping changes in the styles of painting and architecture. At the same time, individuals emerged as known artists rather than unnamed craftsmen.

Anonymous

At the start of the medieval period, artis[ts] were seen as just another type of craftsman, like builde[rs]. Most did not sign their work.

FATHER OF GOTHIC ARCHITECTURE

+ Abbot Suger's new style

The Gothic style arrived in Europe in the 1100s. It used pointe[d] arches, **vaulted** ceilings, and stained glass. The first Gothic-style building was Saint Denis near Paris. Abbot Suger of Sain[t] Denis realized that his church needed many repairs. Instead, i[n] 1137 he hired architects to transform his church into a grand, Gothic cathedral. It still stands today (left).

BREAKING NEWS

The Italian painter, sculptor, and architect Giotto di Bondone is making his name with a new approach to painting. His method is more natural and realistic than previous painting styles. Even in his religious scenes (right), people look lifelike. There are real-looking landscapes in the background. In the early 1300s, Giotto painted three sets of frescoes in churches in Assisi, Padua, and Florence. They look set to change the world of art forever!

THE ILLUMINATOR

- ☞ French master
- ☞ Drawings for the queen

Jean Pucelle was a talented French illuminator. His most famous work is a *Book of Hours* commissioned by the French queen, Jeanne d'Evreux. This tiny, personal prayer book includes 25 full-page paintings and almost 700 illustrations in the margins. The paintings are religious scenes. The drawings show ordinary French people, as well as real and imaginary animals.

ARTIST AND ENGINEER

✦ Brunelleschi can do it all!

The architect Filippo Brunelleschi didn't only rely on artistic talent to design the Duomo in Florence. He also used engineering skills by inventing machines to lift the heavy materials. Builders completed the dome in 1436, and topped it 10 years later with a marble turret, also designed by Brunelleschi.

LEONARDO SEES THE FUTURE

+ A Renaissance man

Leonardo da Vinci (right) was born in Italy in 1452. He became one of the greatest painters of all time. His most famous works are the *Mona Lisa* and *The Last Supper*. However, he was also fascinated by science, nature, and engineering. Leonardo had ideas for inventions that were far ahead of his time. They included a parachute and a helicopter.

The Great Thinkers

Philosophers are people who study the meaning of life, knowledge, truth, and other ideas. The medieval world produced some remarkable thinkers whose writings are still studied today.

CHRISTIAN CONVERT

+ **St. Augustine writes his memoirs**

+ **Describes conversion to faith**

Aurelius Augustinus, or St. Augustine, was born in 354 in what is now Algeria. At age 33, he became a Christian and devoted his life to preaching and writing. Augustine read the work of classical philosophers, such as Plato. He tried to combine their ideas about the world with Christian thinking. St. Augustine's most famous work, *Confessions*, describes his **conversion** to Christianity.

Did you know?

Scholasticism is a way of thinking that started in the Middle Ages. It was based on the teachings of early Christians and the work of the classical philosopher Aristotle.

A PERSONAL PHILOSOPHY

✦ **Thomas Aquinas studies Aristotle**

Thomas Aquinas was an Italian monk in the 1200s. He studied the writings of the Greek philosopher Aristotle, who wrote about reason and logic. Aquinas, who was deeply religious, developed his own philosophy. He tried to bring together the beliefs of his own Christian faith with Aristotle's ideas about reason.

MY MEDIEVAL JOURNAL

Christine de Pisan wrote ballads to earn money. Ballads are long poems that tell a story in a series of many short, rhyming verses. Try writing your own ballad about a recent event in your life or about an event on the TV news.

POWERFUL WORDS

- ☞ **Celebrating women**
- ☞ **Writing for money**

The Italian writer Christine de Pisan grew up in France, in the court of Charles V. She was widowed at a young age and started writing ballads to earn money for her family. In the early 1400s, de Pisan turned to more serious writing. She was greatly interested in politics and women's rights. Her most famous work is *The Book of the City of Ladies*. It celebrates the historical achievements of women.

SCOTTISH SCHOLASTIC

◆ **The nature of existence**

Born in Scotland, John Duns Scotus became a Franciscan friar in 1291. Duns Scotus studied **theology** at Oxford and later lectured at the University of Paris. Duns Scotus was a Scholastic. The Scholastics studied by looking at opposing arguments. They wanted to make it possible to have faith in God, but also to use reason to understand the world. Duns Scotus tried to figure out how the will of individuals was related to the will of God, which the Bible said controlled the world.

I've Got an Idea!

Medieval inventors used science, engineering, and math to come up with innovations that changed the way people understood the world around them. Their ideas still help to shape the world today.

BANG! BANG! BOOM!

✦ **Gunpowder reaches Europe**

✦ **Changes nature of warfare**

Gunpowder originated in China in the late 800s. The Chinese began to use it in firearms in the late 1200s. Gunpowder reached Europe in the early 1300s. Europeans started using gunpowder in cannons. That changed the way medieval wars were fought. Cannons could destroy the walls that protected castles and cities.

BENEATH THE SKIN

☛ **How the body works**

☛ **Cutting open cadavers**

In the early Middle Ages, few people understood human anatomy. The Muslim scientists Al-Razi and Ibn Sīna started to learn how the body worked. By the 1300s, Italian universities allowed medical students to cut open and study cadavers, or dead bodies. Leonardo da Vinci **dissected** corpses to create accurate drawings of the workings of the human body (right).

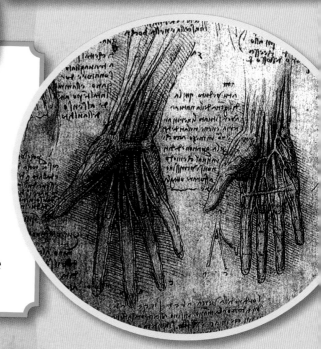

NEWS FROM AFAR

The Chinese invented the **compass** around the 200s. They used a spoon-type device to indicate the direction of north. Medieval Europeans adapted the compass to make it more useful for sea navigation. Around 1300, the Venetians used a magnetized pin to create the mariner's compass. The needle turned to point to the north. The new device helped European explorers setting off across the oceans to find distant lands.

HORSE POWER

+ Small inventions...

+ ...large rewards

The horse collar and horseshoe are small inventions that made a major difference. They enabled horses to become more useful. The horseshoe protected their hooves, making the animals less likely to slip. The collar distributed the weight evenly when the horse was pulling a heavy cart or plow (below). This enabled farmers to plow rougher ground, and merchants to transport heavy goods more quickly.

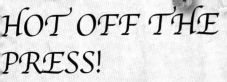

HOT OFF THE PRESS!

✦ New version of Chinese original

The Chinese invented **moveable type** for printing. In Europe, Johannes Gutenberg was the first person to use metal type in a printing press. Around 1455, Gutenberg created the first printed Bible. His metal letters could be arranged into a page of words, then reused for other pages. This made it possible to make many copies of books more easily. Gutenberg made between 160 and 180 copies of his Bible. In time, his invention made books available to everyone.

Glossary

altarpiece An artwork displayed on the altar of a church

calligraphy Decorative handwriting

compass A device for indicating north used for navigation

conversion The act of adopting a new religion

dissected Cut open for medical study

effigies Sculptures or models of people

epic A long poem about heroes from the past

flying buttresses External struts used to support the walls of a cathedral

geometric Having regular lines and shapes

humanism A way of thinking that puts more importance on human reason rather than on biblical teaching

legendary Describes something said to have happened in the past for which there is no solid evidence

literacy The ability to read and write

lyrics Poems about the writer's feelings

manuscripts Documents written by hand

mosques Muslim places of worship

moveable type Letters carved on individual blocks of wood or metal and used for printing

orders Societies of monks or nuns who follow particular rules

patrons People who pay for works of art or encourage artists and performers

perspective A means of making objects on a flat surface appear three-dimensional

philosophy A set of ideas about life and thought

pilgrims People who travel to sacred places for religious reasons

plainchants Sacred songs sung without the accompaniment of any musical instruments

poet laureate An official poet who writes poems for special occasions

Purgatory In Christian thought, a place where souls go after death to be purified

Renaissance A period in Europe seen as a rebirth of culture

romances Medieval poems about the deeds of knights

scribes People who copy out documents

sonnets Formal poems of 14 lines

tapestries Wall hangings of woven textiles

theology The study of religion

vaulted Arched

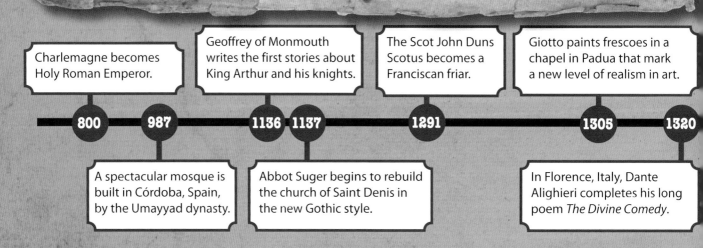

Charlemagne becomes Holy Roman Emperor.

Geoffrey of Monmouth writes the first stories about King Arthur and his knights.

The Scot John Duns Scotus becomes a Franciscan friar.

Giotto paints frescoes in a chapel in Padua that mark a new level of realism in art.

800 **987** **1136** **1137** **1291** **1305** **1320**

A spectacular mosque is built in Córdoba, Spain, by the Umayyad dynasty.

Abbot Suger begins to rebuild the church of Saint Denis in the new Gothic style.

In Florence, Italy, Dante Alighieri completes his long poem *The Divine Comedy*.

On the Web

medievaleurope.mrdonn.org/cathedrals.html
An introduction to medieval cathedrals, how they were built, and their important place in medieval life.

www.ducksters.com/history/renaissance.php
This website has many links to pages about the Renaissance and the artists who worked at the time.

www.coolkidfacts.com/leonardo-da-vinci-facts/
A page of fascinating facts about the first "Renaissance Man," Leonardo da Vinci.

www.bbc.co.uk/history/historic_figures/chaucer_geoffrey.shtml
A biography of the poet Geoffrey Chaucer from the BBC History website.

Books

Cels, Marc. *Life in a Medieval Monastery.* (Medieval World). Crabtree, 2004.

Delaware, Steven S., and Giovanni Di Pasquale, and Matilde Bardi. *Art and Culture of the Medieval World* (Ancient Art and Cultures). Rosen Central, 2010.

Macdonald, Fiona. *You Wouldn't Want to Work on a Medieval Cathedral!: A Difficult Job That Never Ends.* Franklin Watts, 2010.

Murphy, Lauren, and Rupert Matthews. *Art and Culture of the Renaissance World* (Ancient Art and Cultures). Rosen Central, 2010.

Nardo, Don. *Leonardo da Vinci* (Eye on Art). Lucent Books, 2012.

Nardo, Don. *Medieval European Art and Architecture* (Eye on Art). Lucent Books, 2012.

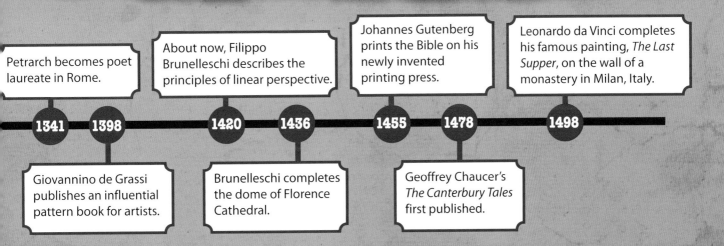

Petrarch becomes poet laureate in Rome.

About now, Filippo Brunelleschi describes the principles of linear perspective.

Johannes Gutenberg prints the Bible on his newly invented printing press.

Leonardo da Vinci completes his famous painting, *The Last Supper*, on the wall of a monastery in Milan, Italy.

1341 **1398** **1420** **1436** **1455** **1478** **1498**

Giovannino de Grassi publishes an influential pattern book for artists.

Brunelleschi completes the dome of Florence Cathedral.

Geoffrey Chaucer's *The Canterbury Tales* first published.

Index